THE OZ CLAN

A new play by Jeff Barstock

THE OZ CLAN

AUTHOR CONTACT INFO:

Tel.: (718) 668-2705
Address:
Jeffrey Barstock
160 Bath Ave.
Staten Island, N.Y. 10305-1430

Any misspellings in the script are intentional, for dramatic purposes.

Lulu Publishing
www.lulu.com

1st Edition: September 2011
ISBN 978-1-105-05420-4

DEDICATION

This play is dedicated in love to God who in helping us grow or unfold
to be all we're destined for through our experiences,
gives us all we basically need to survive,
and with thanks to Chris Dulabone who painstakingly typed up the script.
He is an Emerald City diamond.
The author also acknowledges L. Frank Baum, whose wonderful
story helped inspire this work.

CHARACTERS:

VORTEX (*Female*)

TASH (*Female*)

LEEVUH (*Female*)

DAYJ (*Female*)

COLT (*Male*)

FOH (*Male*)

LECK (*Male*)

ZARNEY (*Male*)

SCENE ONE:

FLAMESTAR—an arts center for seniors in Brooklyn New York; specifically the small main activity room early afternoon on a spring day in 2010. There is an empty worktable at center with vacant chairs beneath as well as closed cabinets. The skyblue walls that are emerald green in spots or possibly the hue of new unfurling pale spring leaves are adorned in places with vibrant framed or unframed artwork and little shelves on which there is unusual creative sculpture and crockery all of which has obviously been conceived by the center's members. There is a fairly large uncovered but closed clear window (stage left) in one of the walls. Through it can be seen outer trees and some sun perhaps. Its shade has not been drawn. The one and only door to the room is closed in the wall opposite the window as light comes up on the otherwise unoccupied space. Almost immediately afterward the door swings open violently for the entrance of VORTEX—a decently if not exactly tastefully dressed slim 65 year old woman—fairly nice looking who has her hand on the knob while shouldering her huge pocketbook. She slams the door shut behind her, drops her bag on the table, marches over to the window, stands before it and shouts;

VORTEX (*Booming*):

I HATE THE SUN!
I HATE BIRDS!
I HATE THE TREES!
I HATE THE SKY!
I HATE CLOUDS!
I HATE SQUIRRELS!
--HATE RAINBOWS!
--HATE EVERYTHING!—

(*Not booming;*)

Especially on a beautiful spring day like this—God.—**Your** day because all it does is mock me, so take such glorious nature and everything that goes with it and leave me in peace.

[*With that, VORTEX angrily pulls down the shade. As soon as she does, COLT enters carrying his art portfolio. He is a darkly blue eyed handsome if rough looking 70 who is nicely dressed like a professional cowboy who is on his day off. He speaks to VORTEX now in a gruff deep if friendly slightly Texan tone which is his usual way of talking or conversing.*]

COLT (*To VORTEX*)**:**
Hey babe—what's the commotion?
(*Puts his portfolio on table.*)
From where I stood outside, it sounded as if a twister just blew through here!

VORTEX (*Sweetly*):
Yes. My mother didn't name me 'Vortex' for nothing. She knew what I was "**destined**" for in the wake of certain—how shall I put it?—"Little challenges". But if I have any more of them, I'll do something that'll give new meaning to the word "**CARNAGE!**"

COLT:
What happened?

VORTEX:
Other than my possibly being evicted now from my apartment and getting mugged, my husband walking out on me, my son marrying a shiftless bellydancer while a new neighbor refuses 'twentyfourseven' to turn down the volume on his stereo to anything lower than what breaks the sound barrier enough to cause even Helen Keller to rise from the dead while a flakey snafu in my bank account caused my direct deposit social security to be virtually non-existent. I was just also nearly savagely inhaled by a cute "**PIT BULL**" among other delights. Otherwise nothing at all really. And **"YOU?"**

COLT:
You're getting hit by a stampede I guess.

VORTEX:
A nice understatement 'Pecos-Bill' 'neath that ten gallon hat of yours. Anymore **brilliant** insights?

COLT:
Sheesh! Any chance that the dog who nearly chomped yuh took possession of your soul? Everything'll work out darlin'. You'll **see**. When life throws us curve balls, flowers come up at least eventually. That's how rain works.

VORTEX:
Naturally.—since I'm pushing up daisies **RIGHT NOW**!

[*Enter TASHEETHA..TASH for short, 72, carrying a shopping bag. She is slightly plump, somewhat pretty and dressed in a vibrant floral pattern.*]

TASH (*Exuberantly*):

Isn't this a bright, wondrous day? Robins singing! Butterflies, lilacs and tulips everywhere!—So much alive and blooming in more than one way it puts the invention of technicolor to shame since God unlike us is of course the **ultimate** artist!

VORTEX (*To her*):

You're flirting with death.

TASH (*As she puts her bag on table*):

Why behead me Vortee? You in a bad mood?

COLT (*Pointedly. Glib.*):

Does Saniflush disinfect toilets?

TASH:

Anything a toilet does has no claim on a lovely day like this. Now Vortee—what is it? You must tell me at **once** so we can fix the problem to leave you free to revel like the inner child you are in this sunlit testament to all the power of nature.

VORTEX (*Shaking her fist at her*):

You want to truly see nature's force? Just keep it up!

COLT (*To VORTEX*):

Cap your squall, Vort. **I'll** settle this. Listen Tash, she hasn't exactly been skippin' down the garden path lately the way buds've been unfolding for her. She's immersed in a kind of grief that isn't so easily extinguished by just a bit of sunshine.

TASH:

What grief?

VORTEX:

Not exactly like that of someone lost to the death of a loved one but I don't want to verbalize it again after telling Colt. It only makes me ill.

TASH:
Anything I can do?

VORTEX:
Not really. I just have to weather things myself—at least for now.

TASH:
Listen Vort..The whole human race surrounds us as God planned it because no-one's meant through anything to fend always only for themselves, so why don't you tell me what's going on. Let's all sit so you can rap to me. We're all early for the workshop anyway, so come-on. Spill the beans. Sit down with me. Talk. Colt, you sit too.

[*They all sit at table.*]

VORTEX (*to TASH*):
I've the kind of troubles you can't resolve. Understand?

TASH:
Try me.

VORTEX (*sighing*):
For one thing I'm about to be tossed out of my pad while my son is taking up with "Sheheruhzahd"—or to be more explicit—a certain belly dancer.

TASH:
That's but a passing fancy. What else?

VORTEX:
Isn't that enough?—Not to mention that Tark left me high and dry while I'm having trouble getting my Social Security! Tark walked out on me.

TASH:
When was this?

VORTEX:
Last week.

TASH:
He'll come back.

VORTEX:

No he won't. He said that he was in love with another woman and that he couldn't stand living with me anymore.

TASH:

What a cliché! After all this time? Out of the blue?

VORTEX:

That's right. Maybe he never really loved me in all these years and just felt obligated to stay with me. I don't know. Anyway—my landlord wants a big rent increase and I can't pay it.

TASH:

Tark just left you stranded, huh?—With no real means for you to take care of yourself.

VORTEX:

Yes.

TASH:

The creep. Men can be real louses sometimes.

VORTEX:

Don't I know it.

TASH:

No offense to you, Colt.

COLT:

None taken. I feel bad about it—about what happened to you, Vort. You have my empathy.

VORTEX:

Thanks, Colt.

COLT:

Don't mention it.

TASH:

Listen, Vort—No matter what happens, you won't wind up in the street. You can always move in with me. I'll share whatever I have with you.

COLT (*To VORTEX*):

I'd offer you my place too if you would want that but if in that scenario you expose yourself accidentally to me, we may both turn assorted colors.

VORTEX:

I appreciate it, Colt—but no thank you, though listen..You're a sweetheart Tash but if ever I take you up on your offer, we may not get along. Even before Tark left me, me and him had trouble sometimes. I'm not the easiest person to live with.

TASH:

Listen honey—after some of the things **I've** been through and after knowing you who I've come to cherish since we've been in this workshop, it'll be a cakewalk for me, **believe** me. Smooth sailing! I've been through stuff that makes the holocaust look like a *Barney* episode. There's no need for me to mentally resurrect it, but the one thing I've learned from it is that when you look up the word "resilience", you see my picture. And besides, I've plenty of room. I've got a spare bed.

VORTEX (*Reluctant*):

I don't know, Tash..

TASH:

Where will you live then on no real funds? In your son's love-nest with "Sheheruhzahd"?

VORTEX:

He's marrying her.

TASH:

A belly dancer? Considering Tim's sensibilities, God only knows why. It's probably lust.

COLT:

Maybe not. He might be seeing something in her beyond that. Not every man's heart is in his groin you know!

VORTEX:

I appreciate such pearls of wisdom, Colt. Yes, according to Tim she's a brilliant poet, but in spite of what you said, I doubt there's anything more to that than her poetic belly-jiggles.

COLT:

I can't say, but as the old maxim goes—"Appearances can be deceiving."

VORTEX:

You're probably right. Actually I don't know the girl that well. All I know is Tim's no idiot. He thinks before he acts. At least he didn't lie to me about her..although I might as well have been hit with a rock when I discovered her "profession" from him.

TASH:

What's her name?

VORTEX:

You mean "Sheheruhzahd"?

TASH:

Her **real** one.

VORTEX:

Valla.

TASH:

That has a nice ring to it. It makes me think of vikings. A viking bride.

VORTEX:

Yeah. Let's hope she's no looter. He's in love with her.

TASH:

You could do worse. You could have a daughter-in-law who's a terrorist that moonlights as a juggling wise-cracking trapeze artist.

VORTEX:
One who never stops talking or smoking long enough to breathe.

TASH:
Or worse—one who's such a bad cook she burns water. Can Valla cook?

VORTEX:
Tim's **heart!** She cooks it very well, but otherwise I don't know. He hasn't mentioned anything to me. Being a belly dancer, I suppose she makes a lot of Indian stuff you eat with your fingers. Finger food.

TASH:
Olives forever.

VORTEX:
On leaves.

TASH:
Indian food's a hit with vegetarians. Is Tim vegetarian?

VORTEX:
No. But he loves animals, so he'd probably go that route if he knew how to without compromising his physical strength. The diet has to be balanced somehow. Yes. When I initially envisioned her, I thought **him unbalanced** for even wanting to marry her. Remember Joan Crawford in "*Baby Jane*"?—When she dragged herself to the bottom of the stairs to get to the phone?

(*As Crawford—desperately.*)

"But **doctor** you don't understand! She's **UNBALANCED!**"

COLT:
Yeah. That was a good flick. Gays love that movie! You can't be a self-respecting gay man and not love *"Whatever Happened to Baby Jane"*. It's a misogynist's dream.

TASH:
Why do they love that film so much?

COLT:

I don't know. I think it's because they "get off" on middle-aged women utterly destroying each other because of all the nasty, overbearing mentally castrating mothers gay men have, so they love to imitate Davis in *"Jane"* who says things to Crawford like—

(*as Davis;*)

"Don't be **stupid**! If you starve you **die!** You really must be **sick!**" You recall Betty twisting Crawford's mind there to torment her. Gays go nuts for that! I'm not gay but I can empathize with where they're coming from while my own mom was a peach so I never had that problem. I miss her to this day—my mom—whom I dream of in sleep and at times secretly weep over.

VORTEX (*Empathetically*):

You really loved your mom.—Didn't you, Colt! You still do.

COLT:

Yeah.

VORTEX:

How old were you when she died?

COLT:

Twenty-eight. She passed from a freak heart attack. For awhile because of that I was mad as hell at God, we were so close. But I didn't feel the same over my dad's death since he was brutal to me, but I forgave him eventually anyway since he couldn't help what he was. We **all** can't, regarding ourselves in a basic sense, though as to mortality..When we gotta go, we gotta go since we weren't designed at least physically to live forever but instead are in God's hands. Yep. I believe in a Heaven and in God's mercy. So as eternal soul, we'll **all** be fine in the end like my pop is. I know that.

VORTEX:

I do too.

COLT:

Anyhow, Tim isn't the only one who loves animals. I do also but I can't picture myself a vegetarian. I'm no rabbit that lives on nothing but greens. I can't do that. I eat meat..so as much as I love animals I guess that when I get

COLT (*Cont'd*):

to Heaven if I make it there, there won't be animal friends for me. I know some **real** animals though. The two legged kind. Know what I mean?

VORTEX:

Oh yes. Some people can be despicable but not all of them.

COLT:

You're right.

TASH:

That's true.

VORTEX:

My mother was an angel though. I loved mine just like you did yours, Colt. So I really missed her when she died. She dreaded my wild side but was always supportive of me in spite of any discipline she doled out. She always encouraged me. But many people after she was gone treated me badly..horribly so I had a rotten streak. It just developed in me.

COLT:

That's understandable. Discipline doled out by parents is important but it should be done in a loving way that brings out the best in their brood..their inner gifts particularly through encouragement. That's what we all should do for eachother. Give eachother love.

VORTEX:

Absolutely. Not to change the subject but I came here today in spite of my problems or due to them because you're my friends whom I needed to be near to distract me. This is an art workshop where we all create. Not destroy if it can be helped.

TASH:

If it can be. Yes.

VORTEX:

Sometimes destructiveness can't.

TASH:

No.

VORTEX:
It depends on the situation.

TASH:
Right.

COLT:
But we should always try our best not to be destructive no matter what the circumstances.

VORTEX:
Yes. It's chaos. Bad. But I have a meanstreak. I know it. The causes are complicated. I don't want to go into them. Yet I'd be different if I could be. I really would.

TASH:
To an extent that's true for us all.

COLT:
Yep.

VORTEX:
Anyway..If Valla can cook, I wonder if she belly dances simultaneously.

TASH:
I wouldn't be surprised. Knowing Tim he wouldn't want to land himself in a dull marriage.

COLT:
Good. Boredom can be lethal.

VORTEX:
True. Well we'll see. We'll see how it goes with them or at least **I** will. I do want the best for my son. That's all I know. No matter what I think, if she makes him happy, that's all I care about.

TASH:
A mother's true words.

VORTEX:

As a mom I can only do my best whatever it is. What time is it? Does anyone have a watch? Mine broke. That's another thing!

TASH (*Checking her own*):

A bit past two.

VORTEX:

The others should arrive at any moment—so why don't we take our projects out?

COLT:

Sounds great!

[*The three start to remove their projects from what they upon entering, carried them in. COLT removes a painting from his portfolio. TASH takes out a half completed sculpture she started on from her bag and VORTEX pulls out a needlepoint work with different threads and a needle from her own.*]

TASH:

Let me see your painting, Colt. What are you working on?

COLT (*Holding it up*):

A lion walking through a far-off galaxy. These are stars and comets—and these here on the side are far-off planets.

TASH (*In observation*):

How cosmic and natural at once. I suppose the universe could be a jungle for lions. Anything can happen in it. Just like anything can in the jungle. Would it be too trite for me to add then that life can be a jungle? Yours is really coming along though. I love all the colors. I think it'll make a great piece!

COLT:

Thanks.

VORTEX:

Can **I** see it?

COLT:

Sure! (*Shows it to her.*)

VORTEX:

The lion looks brave, kind and noble sort of like Aslan in the C.S. Lewis novel series.

COLT:

Oh—you mean that lion who represents Christ? Yep. I know him. I read almost all those books concerning the White Witch and all.

TASH:

Noble. Yes. You're right, Vortex.

COLT:

I guess I wanted him to be that way here. I always wanted to be noble, kind and brave but wasn't always. At times I've been a coward instead. A cowardly lion.

VORTEX:

Colt, we've all been that at one time or other..more than I'd care to admit. It's human though.

TASH:

Yes. But then there are moments we show courage—when we're really tested just like the Cowardly Lion was. I'm sure there are times Colt when you prove yourself very brave.

COLT (*Softly*):

Maybe.

[*The door opens again and DAYJ enters. She's a tough looking but lovely 74 year old black woman in a nice simple outfit. She carries a large paper bag.*]

DAYJ:

Good afternoon all! That big old fireball in the sky is shining so brazenly, it's fit to be tied! God wasn't asleep at the wheel when He formed it. No **sir**!

(*She puts her bag on table.*)

Are all you works of art chomping at the bit to turn out art?

VORTEX:

The only thing that's turning or grinding, Dayj, is my son's fiancé! He took up with a belly dancer!

DAYJ:

Lord have mercy! Let's hope then that there's more goin' on inside their heads than what happens nightly around her **stomach**.

COLT:

You take the cake, Dayj. It's an experience knowing you.

DAYJ:

I should hope so. I wouldn't want to spend the rest of my days being otherwise. I was born to tapdance in all ways, but hopefully and certainly not intentionally on any soul. That's not kind—God knows.

[*DAYJ sits. LEEVUH, 64 now enters dressed for spring in soft pastels. She has pleasant features that reflect the ghost of her lost childhood. For, she was once the belle of the ball in her past resplendent beauty but she somehow remains still a flower..a blossoming one of hazel eyes and slightly silvering hair. She carries a pretty shopping bag.*]

LEEVUH:

I'm here—here—here! Sorry I'm late. My bus broke down.

DAYJ:

You're never too late, sugar to bring beauty into the world. For, you certainly are one!

LEEVUH:

Dayj, if flattery was currency, you'd put even Atlantic City out of business.

TASH (*To LEEVUH*):

I don't want to get on the praise bandwagon but that new outfit becomes you.

LEEVUH:

Of course! I have to do **some**thing to adorn what's left of me.

DAYJ:

You **stop** that! That's false modesty!—Blackmailing folks to feed you compliments. Now you sit down and behave or I'll **really** recall your youth by giving you a sound spanking!

LEEVUH:

You promise? I've been having such trouble with my memory lately—that doing so would prompt an oxygenated bloodflow to my brain.

DAYJ (*Playfully*):

Just sit and be quiet!

LEEVUH (*Playing along*):

Yes mother.

(*She sits and places bag beside her on floor.*)

So how's everyone? Particularly **you**, Colt—you wild steed.

COLT:

I'm nothin' less, my dove..A mustang rearin' to go. Care for a ride?

LEEVUH (*Like a little girl*):

Cowboys are my fantasy.

VORTEX:

Here only two seconds and already she's flirting.

COLT:

Time waits for no woman or man for that matter.

DAYJ:

You got that straight. Time hasn't the time for such nonsense some**TIMES**.

LEEVUH:

Where are the other men? I need them—those cuties. Art has no place in a menless world.

COLT (*Playfully*):

I'm not enough of one for you?

DAYJ:

Pay her no mind, Colt. She's fickle—but if she doesn't cut it out, I'll see to it that her fantasies take on the form of pain induced hallucinations.

LEEVUH (*To her*):

Some friend **you** are! The world is rife obviously with nothing but illusion!—False friends!

COLT:

I'll drink to that and I don't drink.

DAYJ (*To her*):

False friend? Leevuh, do I owe you anything less than the truth especially regarding your courting practices? Anyhow—as Colt here would say—'They should be moseying in here' anytime now.

LEEVUH:

The other men or illusions?

VORTEX:

Is there a difference?

[*Now LECK enters in casual spring clothes that include shorts. He's a fragile 75 who is carrying an umbrella and a satchel of some sort.*]

LECK:

It didn't rain. The weatherman makes mistakes so I expected rain.

VORTEX (*Dully*):

You **always** expect rain, Leck.

LECK:

That's **right**! You can't be too careful. That's why I always carry my umbrella. It's my sword against sneaky downpours as well as would-be muggers. Any of 'em come near me, I'll crack 'em good with this thing 'til they see more light than what twinkles on Christmas. Nope. You can't trust those weathermen nor mother nature—that **harlot** who'll drown you soon as look at you when your head's in the clouds. You won't catch **me** gettin' wet!..No **m'am**! Not me. Not with **my** trusty umbrella.

DAYJ:

What d'you think will happen if Heaven forbid you **do** get wet, Leck? You think you'll dissolve like Alkaseltzer?

LECK (*Angry*):

That's **NOT FUNNY!!** Getting wet is nasty business. A disaster. I can come down with all kinds of diseases. You better watch out young lady. You just make sure **you** don't get sick when **you** get rained on. Yeah..drenched in the pouring rain!

DAYJ:

But you take showers and don't get sick. I know you do because you're always clean.

LECK:

You think you're real smart, don'tchyuh? But I take **WARM** showers. **WARRRMM SHOWERS!!!—Betty Boop!!** You can't get sick from a warm shower.—a word from the wise. You take cold ones?—Ice cold showers? **Do you**?—Even in **summer**?

DAYJ:

No.

LECK:

Well there you go! A blow for **me**!

LEEVUH (*Smiling*):

How are you, Leck Darling?

LECK:

Dry as toast and never better, though my rheumatism plays the devil with me now and then. How are you, Lee?

LEEVUH:

Other than my occasional bouts with athritis? Fine.

LECK:

Arthritis can cripple you. Sorry about that. I hope you feel better.

LEEVUH:
It's not that bad. I'll live. You bring in your project today?

LECK:
Sure did! It's in my satchel here. Now can I give you a kiss?

LEEVUH:
Only if you promise to stop yelling at people. Honey attracts more bees for flower-pollen than vinegar does.

LECK:
Right!

LEEVUH:
You may kiss me then on my cheek.

[*He walks over and kisses her.*]

LECK (*Delighted*):
Hot-dog!

VORTEX:
You stole that from George Bailey in "*It's a Wonderful Life*."

LECK:
If it serves me, who cares? Why you pointing that out, Vort? You jealous? You want a kiss from me too or if I deprive you of one, will you turn into a full blown tornado?

VORTEX:
I might.

LECK:
Well we can't have that.
(*He steps over to kiss VORTEX.*)

VORTEX (*Afterward*):
Sweet.

DAYJ:
Don't **I** rate one?

LECK:
When you remove that whammy about Alkaseltzer.

DAYJ:
You'll never dissolve even in a monsoon. Can I have my kiss then?

LECK:
Yeah. But I draw the line at Colt. Tash, you want one?

TASH:
Don't be silly sweetie. It's not necessary.

DAYJ:
Where's mine?

[*LECK kisses her cheek.*]

That's better. I'll savour it for rainy days.

LECK:
You do that, honey. My kisses keep dolphins dry.

DAYJ:
I've no doubt. Now have a seat, Leck.

[*He sits at table setting down his umbrella and bag as FOHZEEUS enters who is known as FOH. FOH is 74 and is dressed like a distinguished gentleman. He has graying dark hair and is slim. One can tell just by looking at him that he is polished and somewhat sophisticated. He is a bit tall. He carries a closed attaché case.*]

COLT:
How yuh doin' Fohzeeus?

FOH:
Not too well. I don't like hot weather. It withers my inner vines. How are the rest of you?

COLT:
Not bad.

DAYJ:
Peachy.

TASH:
Good.

LEEVUH:
Passable. No, a bit better than that to be honest.

VORTEX:
As for me, I'm distracted for now—thank goodness.

LECK:
Dry as a bone and grateful for it. You never carry an umbrella?

FOH:
Not today. Rain wasn't in the forecast.

LECK:
You can't go by that. Meteorology is fallible.

LEEVUH:
Foh, you look dashing today—but then you always do. Don't you ever get bored with looking wonderful? Ever feel like slumming it?

FOH:
Such isn't in my blood..though I suppose that occasionally breaking from what gives me I confess such a false sense of security—my pattern—might prove refreshing.

TASH:
It would. You should try it sometime. I'm always trying new things in my own way.

LEEVUH:
Yes Foh. Break loose! Slum a bit. Read trash.

FOH:

You don't really mean that, Lee.

LEEVUH:

I **do**! Cultivate an unconventional palatte. Become a beatnik. Adopt the '*Star Trek*' code. Go where 'No-one has gone before'! You've seen *'Star Trek'*. Don't you ever watch television?

FOH:

Not really. For the most part it's a passive activity that promotes mental decay.

LEEVUH:

Lighten up. Oh come on! What-are-you?—a **snob**? You're too nice for that, Foh. Listen—I've got a book in my bag here by Jacqueline Suzanne. It's 'dated' but hey—everything's in it; Lust. Suicide. Corruption. Incest. Gay fetishes. Murder. Rape. Passion. Gluttony. Hot bedroom scenes. Shady politics. The works! I've just finished it. I'll give it to you. Live a little.

FOH:

I'd rather not.

LEEVUH:

You don't want to **live**? What-are-you?-**<u>Depressed</u>**?

FOH:

I don't indulge in that sort of thing. It doesn't resonate with me.

LEEVUH:

How do you know if you've never tried it?

DAYJ:

Oh leave the man alone! He won't traffic in trash!

LEEVUH:

Oh yes he will because I know what's good for him. He needs an antidote to the way he's living now which isn't living at all I suspect.

FOH:

Allright. Give me the book, but I'm not promising you I'll run out to join a commune or nudist colony afterward.

LEEVUH:

Fair enough. Here.

(*She slides it down table to where he's standing. He picks it up.*)

COLT:

Listen Foh—if it proves good, let me have a peek. I'm curious.

VORTEX:

Curiosity kills more than cats.

LEEVUH:

Shame on you, Vortex! It's crucial to keep an open mind. Even ten year old Francie of "*A Tree Grows in Brooklyn*" knew that the way she plunged into a library to broaden her horizons.

VORTEX:

She was fiction.

LEEVUH:

All fiction is somehow based on reality.

DAYJ:

Judging by the way we're heading, I'm beginning to think this group is becoming fiction.

LEEVUH:

Reality can be stranger than that. Don't you know?

DAYJ:

Anyway Foh—grab a seat. That case of yours is carrying your project I suppose.

FOH:

Yes.

DAYJ:
Fine. We'll all start working on our stuff.
(*FOH sits. He opens his case on table as the others reveal their projects.*)

LEEVUH:
But not everyone's here yet.

DAYJ:
You need a full census to give vent to your soul?

LEEVUH:
I guess not.

DAYJ:
Allright then! Gather what you all need in supplies from the cabinets but **please** even though art as love is messy—let's try anyway, shall we?—not to make too much of a mess since my Stepford Wife proclivities only go so far.

[*They all begin working on their art projects assisted by what they take from the surrounding cabinets. Their pieces are of various types including sculpture, needlepoint, yarnwork and ink drawings.*]

VORTEX (*After a beat*):
I want an honest opinion. How do you all think my needlepoint is coming along?

LECK:
Let's see, sugar. Hold it up.

[*She does for their inspection.*]

LECK:
What **is** it?

VORTEX:
What does it look like?

LECK:
Some sort of abstract?

VORTEX:

No. Actually it's a picture of my soul or what I feel my soul truly is at the moment.

LECK:

There's a lot of dark blotches in there. You feel dark?

VORTEX:

At times I do as a consequence of certain things I've weathered or questioned in myself, but when I come up with answers, I don't like what I see in the mirror.

LEEVUH:

Honey,..we've all had those days. Certain things happen to us to dictate choices we make which causes us to perhaps hate ourselves sooner or later but it's not always like that. We also see what's good in us.

TASH:

Yes, since there are bright parts in your needlepoint, Vort. It's vibrantly colorful in aspects like there and there. See?—which shows you recognize what you truly are deep down in spite of what regrettable life choices if any you've been forced to make. Yes—bright parts or light in its threads which indicates all you are truly or want to be or ultimately meant to be..like the 'wait and see tree' Gloria Stump talks about with Opal in that story—"*Because of Winn Dixie*".

VORTEX:

Yes—I know that tale. I loved it. You really see that in my work?

TASH:

Yes.

LEEVUH:

I do too. We all do I think.

COLT:

I see it.

LECK:

Yeah—me too.

FOH:
So do I.

DAYJ:
As **I** do.

COLT:
Yep. There's light and dark in everything. In us all.

VORTEX (*To COLT*):
Being that's so, do you think there's darkness in God, since He made us? He made Satan with what was originally in Him—I mean Satan as soul.

COLT:
Is God dark in part then? I don't know but He's all love. That I do know..even if He **is** capable of great destructive anger. All I know is we couldn't love if He didn't first love us. It's right there in Scripture.

DAYJ:
Amen! Now Colt, can I ask you something?

[*They all continue working on their projects.*]

COLT:
What?

DAYJ:
Why do you see yourself as a cowboy?

COLT:
Because at heart that's what I am.

DAYJ:
Why?

COLT:

I love wild horses and open spaces even though I've never lived that—never slept under prairie stars in the night that at close range are as big to the eyes as quarters.

DAYJ:

Why haven't you?

COLT:

Life! It's a long story. All I can say is I once lived on a ranch as a boy. In Texas. That was where after I was born, my mom named me 'Colt'. I guess she foresaw my love for colts and all horses when in her arms I first knew daylight. I wanted to be a colt myself in fact. Run free. But I didn't have the best childhood. Although my mom was a saint, my dad who thought I'd turn out weak, beat me up all the time though she tried her best to defend me. They used to fight about it but she was a fragile thing so usually lost to him. She loved me a lot and so died young because of that I think—which I had trouble forgiving my father for. I blamed him. But I guess he was just an unhappy drunk who because of something missing inside him I guess, wanted me to be some kind of hero that I couldn't be. I don't know. All I know is that the reason I forgave him is because in that way he couldn't help himself like we sometimes can't help what we are even when bad or weak since it's our basic chemistry. You know? Hero! The only heroic thing I ever did was trying to protect her from him in the face of his frustrated anger. One time I stopped a little kid from running in the middle of traffic and even saved a real cowboy through my blood transfusion—someone I lost touch with..So much for being a hero. I worked as a businessman for my dad most of my life in the city so never had time for anything including getting hitched. I'm alone..but I don't want to go on about my past anymore. It's a painful subject.

DAYJ:

Sorry.

COLT:

No sweat.

LEEVUH:

Through God no-one is truly alone, Colt—but to my mind it doesn't matter if someone is a hero or not or if they don't accomplish great things. All that

LEEVUH (*Cont'd*):

counts is whatever good is in them—what capacity for love or compassion they have—no matter what form that takes, however great or small.

FOH:

I couldn't agree with you more.

DAYJ:

None of us couldn't.

VORTEX:

Absolutely.

LECK:

Yep.

VORTEX:

How's that sculpture coming out, Tash?

TASH:

I don't know. I started wanting to make the head of a woodnymph but it's turning out to be a demon. Oh to heck with this! I'm ready to throw in the towel! I don't want demons in my midst.

LECK:

Turn the head to face us. Let's check it out.

[*She does.*]

TASH:

There! See? The features are all wrong. It looks perfectly evil!

LECK:

It's kind of cute I think.

TASH:

Have you had your eyes examined lately?

LEEVUH:

Oh really Tash! It doesn't look that bad. You just have to work out the bugs, that's all.

TASH:

Bugs! It needs major surgery or an exorcist.

LEEVUH:

Listen..Demons are a part of life.

TASH:

They won't stare at me from **my** shelf!

LEEVUH:

They're in us **all**..demons.

TASH:

So what are you suggesting?—that this "**abomination**" is somehow a reflection of me?

LEEVUH:

What if it is? Accept it. The road to love others is through self-acceptance. If we want to forgive them truly, we need to forgive our own little shortcomings.

TASH:

Forgive me then please if I toss this at your skull!

COLT:

Relax. She meant no harm.

TASH:

But "**I**" do. I'm going to destroy this monstrosity.
(*She glares at the sculpture.*)

LEEVUH:

Don't! It'll be like killing yourself.

TASH:

I'm suicidal!

[*With that—out of frustration, TASH violently wrecks the head.*]

LECK (*To TASH*):
So you think you're a woodnymph—huh?

TASH (*Shouting at him*):
Oh for **HEAVENSAKE!** Can't someone create a work of art without it being construed as the artist's soul?

LECK:
Yep. She thinks she's a woodnymph. Look how mad she's getting. It's not my fault if you can't be one.

TASH:
Why don't you dissolve in the rain?

LECK:
Nope. People can't always get or be what they want. Sometimes even when you put your whole heart into your dream, it doesn't work out since it's simply not meant to. The universe is littered with such broken pieces caused by people usually.

LEEVUH:
Still, I don't think if you really have your heart set on something, you should give up.

LECK:
After a lifetime of noble effort, that's just the kind of epitaph or something like it that will be inscribed on my tombstone. You know what it'll read?—"Don't give up, Leck! You'll win someday." My umbrella here is for **all** kinds of rain, sweetie. Yet the rain just keeps falling. According to winners, you gotta realize your dream or you don't deserve to live. Isn't that stupid?

VORTEX (*Brightly*):
But like Annie said in the musical.."The sun'll come out tomorrow."

LECK:
Ah—**Shuddup!**

[*Enter ZARNEY, 63, who is average looking and sportively dressed. He holds a bag. Shakes himself out.*]

ZARNEY:
You know—it's raining outside.

LECK (*Victorious. To all*):
Hah!—see what I **told-yuh**? And I'm the only one here with an umbrella! I'll betchyuh it's pouring cats and dogs.

ZARNEY:
It is.

LECK:
Just like on gravestones with mocking epitaphs.

ZARNEY:
What do you mean?

LECK:
Nevermind. We've covered that ground. Haven't we Leevuh? Vortex?

ZARNEY (*To him*):
You can be cryptic, Leck. Anyhow—sorry I'm late. I got held up at home.

LECK:
By a gunman?

ZARNEY:
It might just as well have been instead of my nervous, crazy dog! He made a wreck of the house. I had to leave him before that and when I got back, what I saw of his handiwork, made the aftermath of Hiroshima look like a showplace. How's everything going with you guys?

TASH:
I destroyed my head. I have to create a new one.

ZARNEY:
That sounds intriguing. You a drug addict coming off an acid trip?

TASH (*Peeved*):
My **SCULPTURE** Zarney!

ZARNEY:
I see.

DAYJ:
Zarn, you look good. Put on a bit of weight?

ZARNEY:
Yeah..My mom's always feeding me. She's a gourmet.—Eightyfour and going strong. She should have her own cooking show. She tests everything on me who eats anything these days not attached to the wall.

DAYJ:
What's the matter? Frustrations?

ZARNEY:
You could say that. Rain is coming down in my life in more ways than one.

LECK:
Rain plagues everyone!

LEEVUH:
It makes flowers grow and without it we'd die of thirst.

LECK:
Don't you get tired of coming up with answers to everything, you pain in the neck?

LEEVUH:
How can you say that to me after that lovely kiss?

LECK:
I'm fickle.

LEEVUH:
I don't believe that.

LECK:
Suit yourself.

LEEVUH:
You love me and you know it.

LECK:
Well, maybe a little.

LEEVUH:
A "little"?

LECK (*Barking at her*):
Okay—a **LOT**!—But you get on my nerves!

LEEVUH:
What relationship doesn't have its problems?

DAYJ:
It's nice having lovebirds around. So diverting. Is it really pouring out?

ZARNEY:
For now anyway.

DAYJ:
Maybe it'll stop later. Pull up a seat to join us. You bring your project?

ZARNEY:
Right here in this bag. It's debatable though whether I'm making any progress with it. I'm sort of drenched. That downpour caught me suddenly.

DAYJ:
Sit and dry off.

ZARNEY:
Thanks.
(*He sits at table. Puts his bag down.*)

TASH:
I'm starting a new one. I'm getting more clay from the cabinets.

VORTEX:
Another head?

TASH:
Yes.

LECK:
A woodnymph?

TASH:
Perhaps. I'd like to try again.

LECK:
Got your heart set on being a woodnymph—huh?

TASH:
Leave me be! I'll do what I want. I like connecting with nature.

LECK (*Spirited*):
"**Nature**" girl!

TASH:
Will you stop teasing me?

LECK:
I'm having fun.

TASH:
If you need fun, join a circus. That's where you'd be most at home anyway—preferably as chow in the tiger's cage. Oh—I didn't mean to say that. I'm sorry, Leck. Sometimes you don't bring out the best in me.

LECK:
I beg to differ. That crack was pretty good.

TASH:
I'm glad it didn't bother you.

LECK:

Not at all. You **should** be a little feisty sometimes. Consistant sugar is nauseating.

TASH (*Peeved*):

Then I'll try to keep you happy! Now if you'll excuse me..
(*She gets up to check cabinets for more clay as the others converse and work on projects.*)

LEEVUH:

When I first walked in here I asked how everyone was but I'm intuitive, so no-one needs answer.

[*TASH returns with new clay.*]

DAYJ:

I'd like to anyway. Clear the air. It seems to me I've a sharp tongue at times. Lord knows that's no good. He doesn't like that and so I apologize.

LECK:

Listen—Even the saints weren't always saintly. Allow yourself to be human for Godsake!

DAYJ:

Please. Let me me go on. Sometimes I'm nasty because I've got troubles. I know. Who doesn't? But I guess they get my goat at times. For instance..right now I'm knitting this scarf for my grandson who doesn't even like me.—thinks I'm too rough around the edges which I probably am.

VORTEX:

You play with him?

DAYJ:

I want to but he sort of avoids me as if I'm some kind of truth bullit which in my candor I **can** be. I shouldn't be but it was how I was raised..taught always to level with people as God inside us does with us. Still—I could use more sensitivity since I'm like walking sandpaper.

LEEVUH:

He'll come around. You'll see. Don't be so hard on yourself. Dayj, I know you can be rough on people sometimes with your opinions but beneath that you have a gold heart. God's love flows through you.

DAYJ:

You really think so? I'm not too sure.

LEEVUH:

If it didn't, you wouldn't feel so bad..nor be knitting that scarf for your grandson.

DAYJ:

Well even though he isn't crazy about me, I do love him.

LEEVUH:

I know that.

FOH:

Look..It's a positive step in our personal evolution to be giving and loving to souls who don't always love us back.

LEEVUH:

That's right Foh. I've been there. I had such a relationship with my husband before he died. I haven't met the right man since, though Leck shows promise.

LECK:

Do I?

LEEVUH (*Playfully*):

Maybe!

LECK (*Facetious*):

Yippee! There's hope for me.

LEEVUH:

Always! But I have issues regarding the world and life, that I really don't want to go into right now.

FOH:
Whatever they are, I hope you resolve them.

LEEVUH:
Thanks, but I don't know if I can.

COLT:
Don't worry. You will one day.

LEEVUH:
I hope so.

ZARNEY:
And if you can't, there's always the ultimate recourse..Good food.—At least that's what **I** turn to when jobs and my relationship with women don't work out.

VORTEX:
Yes, but food prices today are obscene—so you may wind up starving while trying to comfort yourself.

TASH:
Food's never a lasting comfort. It's just fuel to keep us alive. I've learned that. In fact some people who can't cope, unfortunately kill themselves through it. It's like alcohol.

DAYJ:
It's a shame about those folks. They need twelve step programs—but we've got to change tracks now. We're getting morbid.

LEEVUH (*Trying*):
Allright. Anyone read a good book lately? I love fascinating trash.

FOH:
What you gave me bears witness to it—so we already know as much, Lee.

LEEVUH:
I used to be a librarian, you know?

TASH:
Really?

LEEVUH:
Yes..but now I'm living alone on a pension. What kind of books do **you** normally read?

FOH:
Me?

LEEVUH:
Yes.

FOH:
I love children's books and helping the homeless.

LEEVUH (*To FOH*):
You ever take in a homeless person?—Into your house?

TASH:
What kind of question is that, Lee?

LEEVUH:
I was just curious.

VORTEX:
I already gave you the scoop on curiosity.

LEEVUH:
I've the right to ask anything I want. God gave me free will. So **do** you, Foh?—Take in homeless people?

FOH:
I don't like to talk about what I do regarding them.

LEEVUH:
Then why mention it?

COLT:
You shouldn't be cross-examining him like this.

TASH:
No.

DAYJ (*To LEEVUH*):
Why ask him in the first place? Does the thought of him helping homeless people bother you?

VORTEX:
She probably doesn't help them herself, so is feeling guilty about it.

LEEVUH (*Angry*):
That's a terrible thing for you to say to me, Vortex! The truth is I **do** help them.

VORTEX:
Do you take them in?

LEEVUH:
Do "**you**"?

VORTEX:
I asked you first.

LEEVUH:
That's a "cop-out"!

COLT:
Don't get in a war over this. It's not something to fight over.

VORTEX:
Well she shouldn't be asking him questions like that!

LECK:
Listen..If the man takes in homeless people, he's entitled to if it makes him happy. It's no sin.

LEEVUH:
I didn't say it was.

LECK:
Well then just leave him alone about it!

LEEVUH:
I wish you all wouldn't gang up on me!

COLT:
Let's drop it. So Foh, you like children's books..

FOH:
I shouldn't have mentioned that thing about the homeless. I hope God will forgive me. I wasn't thinking!

LEEVUH:
Don't feel that way, Foh. Helping the homeless in any way is good no matter what the story. The truth is I **don't** take them in—but if you do, you're a wonderful human being even if you do mention it. So what? God understands that we're all human especially when we make mistakes..not that taking in the homeless is one of them but you have to be careful. A lot of them are very sick in different ways.

FOH:
I **try** to be cautious. I just want to serve God. Those people have nothing. I was there myself once. I know what it's like!

VORTEX:
You don't have to defend yourself, Foh. You're a really good soul. I've known that about you for a long time.

FOH:
I know I shouldn't have mentioned it but helping them the way I do gives me a sense of purpose. I lead a very empty life otherwise.

TASH:
Well—you're a lesson in compassion, so your life isn't empty. Doing things to help others in need is very meaningful.

COLT:
Yes. That's what it really means to be a hero.

LECK:
Right.

DAYJ:
He's helping God. Amen!

ZARNEY (*To FOH*):
Just be careful man.

FOH:
I will.

LEEVUH (*To FOH*):
What's that art piece you're working on, Foh?

FOH:
An ink drawing.

LEEVUH:
Of what?

FOH:
A tornado carrying a house with a little girl sleeping inside it.

LECK (*Excited*):
Dorothy? You doin' a drawing from "*The Wizard of Oz*"?

FOH:
Yes. In spite of everything I've ever read, "*The Wizard of Oz*" is my favorite book. Children's fantasy keeps me young. I still read it.

LECK:
Don't that beat all! My Craypah sketch here is from "*The Wizard*" **too**!

FOH:
Is it?

LECK:
Sure! **Look**!
(*LECK shows it to him.*)

FOH:
What's that? The tin man?

LECK:
I must be a bad artist. No other. Can't you tell? But look at **yours**! That's a powerful lookin' cyclone, Foh.—And Dorothy in it appears sweet and gentle. Innocent. Trusting. Is that Toto with her?—Her little dog?

FOH:
Yes.

LECK:
In that house?

FOH:
Right.

VORTEX:
Can **I** see?
(*FOH holds his up for her.*)
Beautiful!

DAYJ:
Let **me** look.
(*FOH shows her.*)
Mercy—isn't that somethin'! You've brought that scene to **life**! I sure do love "*The Wizard of Oz*". I must've seen that film a billion times! Ever since Judy did it, it breaks my heart anytime someone feelingly sings "*Over the Rainbow*".

LEEVUH:
You ever read the novel by Baum, Dayj? **I** did when I was little. I loved the story too. In fact my sketch here is a picture of Glinda.

DAYJ:
No kidding!

LEEVUH:
Nope. See? (*Shows her.*)

COLT:
And mine could be taken for the Cowardly Lion in cosmic terms! Can I see yours, Foh?

(*FOH displays it.*)
That's **great**!

ZARNEY:
You won't believe this but **I've** done one here of the Yellow Brick Road. It's symbolic to me of life's journey. That's what "*The Wizard of Oz*" really is.
(*Displays his.*)

DAYJ (*Like a happy child*):
Oz here everywhere!

ZARNEY:
Though mine isn't too good. It is as I said—a work in progress.

DAYJ:
We **all** are, honey!—So don't sell yourself short. That's a fine road of yellow bricks, Zarn. They shine like the sun as does every step on our individual paths to spiritual unfoldment. No, Leevuh—I never read the book. I wish I had but this is fantastic! All that's missin' is the Wizard, Scarecrow and that bad old wicked witch.

LEEVUH:
Not to mention the Munchkins.

VORTEX:
Those flying monkeys or even the poppy field.

TASH:
And what about Emerald City?

DAYJ:
That **too**! I could sure use those gems on Easter Sunday to adorn my dull outfits.

LEEVUH:

Well dynamic as you are, no matter what you wear, you sparkle underneath like an emerald.

DAYJ:

Thanks baby. Flattery will get you everywhere faster than Dorothy's ruby slippers.

FOH:

In the novel they're silver. Ruby was just an M.G.M. concept. There's a whole history about how pairs of those ruby slippers were stolen and practically killed over.

DAYJ: (*Like an excited child*):

I've got an idea!

LEEVUH:

What?

DAYJ:

Why don't we all get up now out of our chairs and become the story? We can all play different roles, but here's the thing..we draw upon our own lives to spiritually and psychologically recreate it!

LEEVUH:

You mean sort of like an "Oz" psychodrama?

DAYJ:

Exactly! Now come-on all of you—**stand up**! Push the table and chairs back. Help me! We're becoming Oz!

VORTEX:

Are you serious about this?

DAYJ:

Never more so. It's a dull, rainy afternoon. We need a change of pace.

(*She stands.*)

Colt!—You're strong. Zarney too. **Leck**! **Foh**!—move the table. You women can shift the chairs. Just slide everything over. Well, what are you waiting for?—The **Second Coming**? We need to bring out the children in

DAYJ (*Cont'd*):

ourselves who really know how in darkness and light, whatever they contain, to be adventurous. So let's go!

[*They all do as she says..moving the furniture until they have nothing but space to become "Oz" in action.*]

SCENE TWO:

[*As before.*]

LEEVUH:

So who will be who?

DAYJ:

First we need a Dorothy.

LEEVUH:

I can be her.

COLT:

And I the Lion as well as Uncle Henry.

DAYJ:

Leck?

LECK:

The Tin Man.

FOH:

The Scarecrow. I'll be him.

VORTEX:

Considering my ire at times, I'm just right for the evil witch and tornado. I certainly have my **own** vortex.

COLT:

From what I've witnessed of your anger, you're not kidding.

TASH:
I'll be Glinda as well as anyone else that's needed.

DAYJ:
And I'll be the Wizard and Aunt Em.

ZARNEY:
And I'm Toto.

DAYJ:
Let's begin.

[*Their surroundings totally darken. The whole clan moves into darkness except for LEEVUH, ZARNEY and VORTEX who are in light.*]

VORTEX (*Booming*):
I'm full of pain and anger. I come darkly out of the sky wanting to **destroy**! **DESTROY**! I'm a **CYCLONE**!
(*She turns in place slowly with her hands spread out.*)

LEEVUH (*As Dorothy. Like a child*):
Where's Aunt Em? Toto, I'm afraid! Em—where are you? So many times I've felt alone and abandoned in my life with no-one to help me! I don't want to be swallowed up by the dark—but darkness is coming. It's coming.

DAYJ (*As Em. At edge of darkness*):
Dorothy where are you? I want to give you love. Find your way to the cellar out of the dark to us! We're looking for you. Find your way to the cellar!

[*DAYJ moves off into dark. VORTEX keeps turning drawing close.*]

LEEVUH:
I can't. It's too dark. For, there's no more love in this dark world..not abiding lasting love anyway. No more love!

ZARNEY (*As Toto*):
That's not true. Woof! Don't worry, Dorothy. You're with me. You're not alone. **I** love you.

LEEVUH:

Thanks, Toto. Right now you're all I have. I've always loved you too, so don't leave me. People are always rejecting..deserting me—so please don't leave me, Toto.

ZARNEY:

Don't worry. I **won't**!

LEEVUH:

We'll hide under the bed in my little house which has always been home to me—a place in which I've until now known love and safety while this terrible darkness passes. Hopefully the cyclone won't kill us. I pray it won't!

VORTEX (*Booming. Spinning*):

PAINN. I'M IN PAINN!! **I'M DARKNESS**! **DARKNESSSS!!!**

[*VORTEX powerfully moves about LEEVUH and ZARNEY, closing in.*]

LEEVUH:

The wind is shrieking! Blowing! I feel so lost.

VORTEX (*Painfully*):

DARKNESSS!!!

[*ZARNEY and LEEVUH slowly collapse to floor as VORTEX moves slowly, dramatically like a cyclone about their splayed figures. Both ZARNEY and LEEVUH fake sleep. After a short while VORTEX moves off into dark and vanishes.*]

LEEVUH ("*Waking*"):

Toto? Did we survive? Are we dead? It's so quiet. Where are we?

ZARNEY (*As Toto. "Awake*"):

I don't know.

LEEVUH:

I don't think I'm too injured, so let's go outside and see.

[*They both move out of invisible house hand in hand.*]

What a beautiful place. It's very strange looking. Pools, grass and giant vibrant flowers everywhere. Aunt Em once called me her flower. I guess

LEEVUH (*Cont'd*):

we're no longer in Kansas. I'm on my own now I suppose. I wonder if everything here we're looking at is what it seems to be. Things rarely are.

ZARNEY (*As Toto*):

Don't forget, Dorothy. You're not alone. You're with me. **I'm** with you.

LEEVUH:

Animals more than anything reflect God's love, so by being in your company I'm with God virtually.

[*TASH approaches. LEEVUH addresses her.*]

Miss, who are you?

TASH (*As Northern Witch*):

Someone to offer you light while you're trying to find your way even though I myself have in ways been without it. For, I've been hurt and stepped on, deceived, betrayed, exploited, abused and judged. Because of all that I should in bitterness have normally become some cold witch like a part of the North, but I'm not although for now you can call me that—the Northern Witch. This is Munchkinland where dwarfs live. None are about right now. They're hiding. Afraid.

LEEVUH:

Of me and my dog?

TASH:

Yes. You're strangers to them.

LEEVUH:

They shouldn't fear us. Toto is harmless and I'm just a little girl.

TASH:

Well they know from what they've been through that appearances are deceiving at times. But don't worry about them. I know you're only a child with this—your dog. Where do you come from?

LEEVUH:

Kansas..a place of comfort and simple peace until darkness came.

TASH:
What is that? A country?

LEEVUH:
Just a spot I've always thought of as home. A place of love. My name is Dorothy. Where are we now?

TASH:
In Oz.

LEEVUH:
Oz? Where is that exactly?

TASH:
Across the Deadly Desert. There is much that is deadly in life. Is the dog your friend?

LEEVUH:
Yes. Right now he's my only one.

TASH:
Friends can prove false.

LEEVUH:
I know—but not Toto.

ZARNEY:
Woof!

TASH (*To LEEVUH*):
I want to help you get back to Kansas, Dorothy, since arriving here the way you did wasn't your fault.

LEEVUH:
Can you do that? I would be so grateful!

TASH:
That's allright..Well first off you need to know that your house landed on one of our wicked witches. We have evil witches here.

LEEVUH:
Just as in ways we do where I come from.

TASH:
Are they as destructive?

LEEVUH:
Incredibly..but all the personal damage they do isn't always immediately obvious. There's just devastation. You feel it only long after the fact.

TASH:
What monsters!

LEEVUH:
Yes—but they can't help being so. It's just that life combined with who they fundamentally are, does that to them..so if you're one of their victims, you just feel sorry for them.

TASH:
You forgive them.

LEEVUH:
Yes.

TASH:
Well that's good. Just don't be like them.

LEEVUH:
I'm not. I'm doing the opposite.

TASH:
Wonderful! This witch is dead. You see her feet sticking out from under your house?

LEEVUH (*Looking*):
Yes.

TASH:
Now put on her shoes. Go on. Their magic will protect you along with my kiss.

(TASH kisses her forehead.)

TASH (*Cont'd*)**:**
Put them on and don't take them off. Otherwise it could prove dangerous for you. They protect you as I've said especially from a witch here who is even more evil.

LEEVUH:
I understand.
(*LEEVUH mimes getting the shoes and putting them on.*)
Now what?

TASH:
You have to go into Emerald City to see the Wizard. She'll figure out a way to send you home. She's very powerful.

LEEVUH:
Is she in any way evil?

TASH:
No. Just..“different”. Until you see her, try in your travels through this at times dangerous land to be a brave little girl. Allright?

LEEVUH (*Apprehensively*):
Okay.

TASH:
That's good. Nice to have met you Toto.

ZARNEY:
Woof!—Same here.

TASH:
I've got to go now. Goodbye.

LEEVUH:
Wait! How do I get there? How do I find Emerald City?

TASH:
Oh. Follow this road of yellow brick. Here's where it starts.

(*TASH shows her. It's invisible.*)

LEEVUH:
Allright. I hope I won't get lost.

TASH:
You won't if you keep following it. Remember Dorothy..You've every reason to be brave because God is with you as is your friend here.

LEEVUH:
Toto.

TASH:
Yes. Goodbye now.

LEEVUH:
Goodbye.

[*TASH hugs her and then walks off into darkness.*]

LEEVUH:
Well I guess that's it. We'd better begin. The road awaits us. Come-on, Toto.

(*ZARNEY and her begin walking in a circle.*)

Anything can happen to us now but I've got her kiss and these shoes. My path is set.

(*They come up soon upon FOH now in light as the Scarecrow who postures himself as if nailed to a post.*)

Oh look, Toto. A scarecrow! I guess they're not only in Kansas. They have them even here.

ZARNEY (*At FOH*):
Woof! Woof!

FOH:
Please stop. That's almost as mindless or should I say brainless as **I** am. What good is a mind anyway if you can't use it for things that really matter such as giving love? And then there are those who are all brawn and no brain who don't think before they speak or act. If more people through their hearts **did**, this world would be a better place. For example..idle words can be so

FOH (*Cont'd*):

destructive while others can be healing. Intelligent people can do such damage through their mouths, so maybe it's best if I remain without a brain. Silent. I can be sort of innocent then.—But still I want one to do good. Will you help me down little girl? I'm nailed to this post..trapped, or is it that I've trapped myself? I don't know—but I want to be free to somehow in a good way fulfill my potential or to fly free in a sense perhaps like the crows who fly into this field, brazenly eating all the corn because I lack a brain for scaring them off. Yes, it could be that I've trapped myself but will you help me out anyway? Please?

LEEVUH:

Of course!

FOH:

I appreciate that but it may not be so easy. It's not easy to help others who don't really want to help themselves. Do I want to help myself? I don't know! After everything I haven't accomplished and been through I've learned to hate myself. Yes..I think I hate myself. That's just what I think even without a brain. **I HATE MYSELF**!—So I don't deserve to be helped. Don't help me. Go **away**!

LEEVUH (*Gently*):

Oh, there's no reason for you to hate yourself, Scarecrow. Accomplishments don't matter as much as the fact that every soul has great value no matter what the world puts it through even when it nails us up to a post only to scare crows. Every soul is worthy of love including you. You wouldn't even exist as such if that wasn't true. So love yourself. It's important.

FOH:

But all I am is a despicably ugly mindless scarecrow. I'm **nothing** really!

LEEVUH:

No you're not—since you want to use your potential to do good. That shows you have a very good heart and that isn't nothing.

FOH:

Thanks. If I do have a heart, I'd never know it because I haven't a brain—but I want to do good. You're right..So will you help me get one?

LEEVUH:

A brain? We'll see but first I've got to get you down off that paralyzing post. No one can realize their potential if they remain trapped. So—what it gets down to is—you need to help me to help you.

FOH:

Allright. Go to the back of me where I can't reach and pull the nails that are hammered into me out of the post.

(*LEEVUH checks his back.*)

LEEVUH:

I don't see where—?

FOH:

They're on the edges.

LEEVUH:

Right!

(*She frees him and he falls awkwardly to the floor. ZARNEY and her rush to his side.*)

Be careful! Watch it.

FOH:

Just some loose straw.

(*He rises clumsily with their help.*)

Oh thank you! I'm free. **Free**!—So I think I'll dance which is sort of like flying anyway!

(*He leaps about acrobatically.*)

Free as the crows who mock me! What's your name?

LEEVUH:

Dorothy.

FOH:

You can call me Blue. Thanks Dorothy for liberating me!

LEEVUH:

It was nothing, Blue.

FOH:
No. That isn't true.

ZARNEY (*Merrily*):
Woof! Woof!

FOH:
I heard you call your dog "Toto".

LEEVUH:
Yes. He's my friend.

FOH:
You're a nice looking dog, Toto.

ZARNEY:
Woof! Thanks! You're a good looking sort of fella, too.

FOH:
Thanks for saying so, Toto. Can I be your friend too, Dorothy?

LEEVUH (*Smiling*):
Sure!

FOH:
Great! Where you headed?

LEEVUH:
To Emerald City so the Wizard there can send me back to Kansas where I live.

FOH:
Kansas? Where's that?

LEEVUH:
Far away from here.

FOH:
Listen..You think your Wizard could make or give me a brain?

LEEVUH:

I don't know, yet it's certainly worth a try—but I doubt if you need one considering the way you express yourself.

FOH:

Oh—but I **do**! The farmer who made me never gave me one. All I am is straw. Please let me go with you! I won't be a burden since I don't need to eat or anything. Straw doesn't eat or sleep.

LEEVUH:

It would be funny if it did. Come-on! I'd be **delighted** to have you! Are you ready to start off with us?

FOH:

Never more so! It's just that I'm still a bit unsteady on my feet after being nailed up to that post so long.

LEEVUH:

Yes, but you'll be allright. Shall we go?

FOH:

Nothing's stopping us.

LEEVUH:

Then we're off!

[*The three walk in a circle, FOH being somewhat unsteady until they come upon in a light, LECK who by his posture conveys paralysis as the rusted and still Tin Man who holds his closed umbrella up as if it was an axe*.]

LEEVUH:

What's this?

FOH:

I think it's a tin man.

LEEVUH:

A man of tin! Yes.

LECK (*Rusted*):
GRUMMGRAHGREEGRIH!!

ZARNEY:
Woof!
LEEVUH (*Concering LECK*):
What's wrong with him?

FOH:
He's trying to talk I think but can't.

LECK (*Frustrated*):
Voil!

LEEVUH:
What's he saying?

FOH:
His mouth is rusted. I don't know.

LECK (*Louder*):
VOIL!

ZARNEY (*Agitated*):
WOOF! WOOF! WOOF!

LEEVUH:
Shush Toto.

LECK (*Louder. Frustrated*):
VOIL!!
VOIL!!
MY-MEE-VOIL!!

LEEVUH:
"I need oil"? Is that what you're saying?

LECK (*Nodding vigorously*):
YEFF! VOIL!!

FOH:
He wants oil! Where is there—?

LEEVUH:
Oil? Oh—here's a can!
[*LEEVUH finds an invisible oilcan.*]

LECK (*Directing her*):
PEEF-VOIL-MY-MOUFF!

FOH:
He wants you to oil his mouth.

LEEVUH:
Allright.
(*LEEVUH does so with "can".*)

LECK (*Struggling*):
THURRTHEHH—THAFF—Thah..That's a relief! Whoever said "silence is golden" should be shot. Could you please oil the rest of me?—**Please**! Especially my arms.
(*LEEVUH "oils" his arms and the rest. He starts to move.*)
Ah! I feel so much better now. Thankyou!

LEEVUH:
How did you get like this?

LECK:
How do you think? I'm allergic to rain. I rusted. There was a downpour and my umbrella here failed me. It wouldn't open. Uselessly stupid thing! Cheap!
(*He throws it away.*)
Thank goodness you came along when you did or I would've been a statue forever.—but in another sense it wouldn't have made any real difference since it's always raining on me in one way or other. Yes life can be as heartless as I am. I crack jokes and pretend to love, but really I have no heart. The tinsmith didn't give me one even though as the flesh and blood man I was, I once had an actual loving one but that's a long story. All I know is I hate being heartless in what is rapidly becoming a heartless world..or at least it seems so to me. I'd like to think I have a heart though

LECK (*Cont'd*):

since before you both came along with your little dog here, I've tried my best to hurt no living thing while putting on for many folks a good love show in its falseness and clowning as I've said to protect myself so that no-one would know I'm hurting inside from being bereft of a heart. You know it's very important to try your best not to kill or hurt any living thing when you don't have a heart because then you're aware of that as I am.

LEEVUH:

But that proves you **do** have one.

LECK:

I don't think so. I've tested myself inwardly again and again in many situations to see if I'm truly loving and came up short. Short!

LEEVUH:

I've felt the same way about myself when things happened to me to coax me to not be very feeling, but that's human.

LECK:

What's your name?

LEEVUH:

Dorothy.

LECK:

I'm Nick Chopper but you can call me "Nick". Listen, Dorothy—my chest is empty. In spite of everything you've said, I want a heart!—A feeling, loving heart that doesn't only address my reasoning about how I need to behave when I don't have one.

LEEVUH:

Maybe the Wizard can help you. We're going to Emerald City to see her. Would you like to come with us?

LECK:

You think she'll give me a heart?

LEEVUH:

I don't know—but it's a risk worth taking considering how much you want one. Don't you think?

LECK:

Yes. Can I? If there's anything troubling you while we're walking there you can talk to me—all of you. I'm a good listener.

LEEVUH (*Warmly*):

So much for your heartlessness.

LECK:

I can't help how I feel.

LEEVUH (*Smiling*):

Yes. You can't help feeling.

LECK:

Oh stop that! I need a heart—**really**!

LEEVUH (*Resigned*):

Okay. You ready to start out with us? I may as well warn you each. There may be dangers.

LECK:

Then we'll all weather them together. I'll do my best to protect you all.

LEEVUH (*Smiling*):

Definitely heartless!

LECK:

Enough! Let's go.

[*They all walk together in a circle*
into what is a terribly dark invisible forest.]

SCENE THREE:

LEEVUH (*Frightened*):

What a dark forest this is.

[*COLT as the Cowardly Lion jumps out at them hatless and dangerously.*]

COLT (*Savagely. Loud.*):
ROARRRRR! ROARRRRR! ROARRRRRR!

FOH:
Stand back! It's a **lion**!

COLT (*Brutally. Loud.*):
ROARRRRRRRRRR!!!!
(*The travellers move away from him fearfully but he pursues them.*)
I'm gonna rip you into tiny pieces and have you for **lunch**!—or better yet, wolf you down whole. How **DARE** you enter my forest? Well it's **your** hard luck 'cause now you're all gonna **die!** Let's see. Who will I eat first? That little dog makes a nice appetizer. He'll do. Come'ere **Mutt**!

LECK:
What a savage! Stop him!

ZARNEY (*In terror but feisty*):
Woof! Woof!

LEEVUH:
Don't you dare hurt my Toto!
(*She gently slaps COLT.*)

COLT (*Suddenly crying*):
You **HIT** me! Don't you know I'm sensitive?—That I can be hurt very easily? Inside me I'm made of glass. I'm afraid to be attacked..afraid to be hurt. I'm **afraid**! Everything scares me—even my own breath! Chances? I don't want to take risks! That's right—I'm a coward—a coward, okay? Everyone wants me to be a hero..even my father but I'm not! I'm a coward. Therefore go away and leave me alone so I can die in peace. Leave me be.

LEEVUH (*Gently*):
I'm sorry I hit you but I too was afraid, for my dog! Listen lion..now and then we're all cowards. There's a coward in us all. Many things can make us cowardly.

COLT (*Guiltily*):

I know but I'm a lion! A big strong one—so that's shameful. I have no courage! Isn't it horrible to be a lion without any courage? I'm so afraid of life and everything in it that I can't even sleep at night! Dreams? I'm afraid I'll have nightmares! Imagine being afraid even to dream or **not** to!

(*He sobs quietly.*)

FOH:

Maybe the Wizard could help him too, Dorothy.

LEEVUH:

Yes! Listen Lion. Why don't you come with us? We're going to see a wizard who may help you. I'm wearing magical shoes but I don't know how to use their power for that, so come with us. Please. Please, Lion! It's terrible to be afraid all the time. It must be so awful. I know I speak for my friends here when I say we don't want to see you suffer so! I know **I** sure don't.

(*She puts her hand comfortingly on his shoulder as ZARNEY does.*)

COLT (*Tremulously*):

You think that Wizard can really help me?

LEEVUH:

She **has** to..must do **some**thing! The northern witch told me she's very powerful.

COLT (*To LEEVUH*):

You have my deep thanks for this. My name's Fuhbby. Okay—I'll go with you but don't expect much of me—cowardly as I am. I want to be brave. Really. But I'm not.

LECK:

Few of us **are** when tested.

FOH:

True.

ZARNEY:

Yes!

LEEVUH:

Here. Take this handkerchief and dry your eyes. Fear-tears may prevent you from seeing clearly..seeing what good may be in store for you.

COLT:

You're right.

(*He dries his eyes with kerchief and blows his nose.*)

LEEVUH:

Are you ready to come with us?

COLT:

—As I'll ever be.

LEEVUH:

Then let's go on. Emerald City can't be far off.

COLT:

Is that where the Wizard is?

LEEVUH:

Yes.

COLT:

Okay—I'm with you. Just don't desert me!

LEEVUH:

From my own life I know what desertion truly means, so I'd never do that..nor would any of us. Come-on Lion. Let's all hold hands and head down the road. These yellow bricks look like hopefilled sunshine.

COLT:

The forest is dark that we're heading into. It's been frighteningly dark for me my whole life.

LEEVUH:

I know, Fuhbby—but now we have eachother to give us light to see our way through it.

COLT:

Right. Let's go!

[*Hand in hand they all head into the forest dark. They vanish.*]

SCENE FOUR:

[*After a little while, they emerge with light on them again.*]

LEEVUH:

Thank God Lion you saved us from those Kalidahs. I've never seen anything like them!

FOH:

Huge-clawed bears like grizzlies but with the heads of tigers.

LECK:

They would have destroyed us if it wasn't for Fuhbby here! Isn't it amazing how when they attacked us he tore into their necks with his teeth?

COLT:

Yes, but I was afraid. Yet the fear of what they otherwise might have done to you all scared me more.

LEEVUH:

You were wounded though. Let me check your injuries. Here..I'll wash the blood off by this stream. I have a cloth on me. Come close. I have to clean your wounds.

(*COLT draws close to her. She dips an invisible cloth into an invisible stream. "Cleans" him.*)

COLT:

Thankyou.

ZARNEY:

Woof!—Thank **you** for saving our lives..mine and Dorothy's..and for protecting the others.

FOH:
Yes I'm very grateful.

COLT:
I had no choice. You're my new friends..so I needed to stand by you.

LEEVUH:
Even so, I appreciate what you did so much but now that I think of it, they couldn't have hurt me in the end since I'm wearing protective shoes. I'm protected by their magic and by the kiss of the Northern witch. Remember, Lion?—I told you. You saved Toto's life though who would have otherwise died and for that I'm eternally grateful.

LECK:
Fuhbby here put up a real battle! You were very brave! Even though I'm made of tin, it's not that strong against such mighty claws so that without you I might've been clawed to pieces.

COLT:
I did what I could, but believe me I was terrified. I still need courage.

LEEVUH:
"Courage is not the absence of fear but acting in spite of it." Aunt Em once told me that from what she read in a book.

COLT:
Even so I still feel shaky. I only acted for your sakes. I never would have done so for myself. I still can't sleep out of fear, so I want courage.

LEEVUH:
And you'll get it. I'm sure the Wizard will provide it. We've been through a lot of frightening things since we first met you Lion, but look!—I finally see a green glow in the distance.

FOH:
Emerald City!

LEEVUH:
At last! Those terrible woods are behind us now. I wonder what it's like.

ZARNEY:

You think they've got doggie biscuits in there? After all we've been through, I could use a treat! We've never been through so much Dorothy, since I've known you.

LEEVUH:

The citizens must be hospitable, I'm sure, Toto. Otherwise the Wizard wouldn't live there.

ZARNEY:

I hope you're right.

LEEVUH:

Look at all those beautiful poppies in the field before it. We'll simply follow this road through them. The Northern witch was correct. It leads directly to the City gates.

COLT:

Good idea.

LECK:

Let's go!

[*They all begin walking again but very soon LEEVUH stops*.]

LEEVUH:

Oh!

FOH:

What's wrong?

LEEVUH:

I don't know. I feel exhausted all of a sudden. Sleepy. It must be the fumes from those flowers. They're acting like a sedative to stop me from going on.

COLT:

For the same reason, I feel tired too. I can't take another step.

[*ZARNEY collapses to floor.*]

LEEVUH:
Toto's collapsed! It's the **poppies**!

COLT:
..Can't stay awake longer.
(*COLT collapses.*)

LEEVUH:
Lion! Toto! Why is it that so many things which seem wonderful in life at the outset are actually..poisonous?
(*LEEVUH collapses.*)

FOH (*To LECK*):
We've got to wake them! We can't just leave them here!

LECK:
Why weren't **we** affected?

FOH:
Because we're not of flesh!

LECK:
I **was** "once."

FOH:
I know. But help me to try to wake them!

LECK:
Dorothy, come-on—get up! Toto! Lion! They won't move! Won't **wake**!

FOH:
I've got an idea..even though it's a longshot. Dorothy told the Lion that her shoes contain magic. Whatever it is, it mustn't be powerful enough to give you a heart and me a brain or she would've tried that, but maybe they can be used to somehow counteract the poison. I'll remove them from her feet and try something.

LECK:

But if you do the wrong thing, it might kill them all! Though heartless as I am, I couldn't allow that! I couldn't bear it!

FOH:

What choice do we have?—To let them sleep here forever perhaps dreamlessly depriving Dorothy of her true home and the lion of the courage he so needs for whatever must be faced by him in life? And what about Toto?—To never romp nor be happy again. No! No-one was meant to spend their whole lives asleep. That's not life's purpose but instead to be lived fully and passionately as possible. To sleep forever is just another form of death. **DEATH**. A pointless one—and death should never be pointless. I'm taking off her shoes!

LECK:

I'll **help** you!

(*They both remove LEEVUH'S invisible silver magic shoes from her sleeping form.*)

What will you do with them?

(*LECK hands one of them over to FOH.*)

FOH (*Both in hands*):

Please God, let this work!

(*He stares at the shoes.*)

Magic Shoes I ask you in desperation to help us. I call upon your power in the name of love!

(*With that FOH rubs the shoes over LEEVUH, ZARNEY and COLT who then afterward start to stir.*)

It's working. **WORKING**!

LECK:

Thank God!

ZARNEY (*Rising*):

WOOF!—WOOF!—WOOF!

LEEVUH (*Rising*):

I feel as if I've been in a void.

[*COLT rises just a bit groggily.*]

COLT:
What a snooze!

FOH:
You allright, Dorothy?

ZARNEY (*Happily*):
WOOF! Dorothy, you okay? After I passed out I didn't know what would happen. I'd die without you!

LEEVUH:
As I would, regarding you.

COLT:
Is everyone accounted for? It's amazing. I don't feel tired anymore!

LECK:
It was Dorothy's shoes! Blue here used them to somehow wake you all!

LEEVUH:
My shoes?

FOH:
Yes. Through God's help I in someway accessed their power.

LEEVUH (*Happily*):
Good thinking!

FOH (*To her*):
Here they are. You can put them back on.

LEEVUH (*As she does*):
Thanks. Now let's not waste anymore time. We don't want this to happen again. Let's hurry to the gates!
(*They move quickly together in unison across space.*)
We're here! I'll knock.

[*LEEVUH mocks knocking. TASH approaches them.*]

TASH (*In a male tone*):
What do you want?

LEEVUH:
Are you the gate guardian?

TASH:
Yes.

LEEVUH:
Please! We need to see the Wizard. All of us.

TASH:
I'm sorry. That's not possible.

LEEVUH (*Devastated*):
Why?

TASH:
She doesn't see just anyone. She's too important and busy for that. She's the life of the City.

LEEVUH:
But we've **got** to see her! It's crucial. The Northern witch sent me. I'm wearing shoes she gave me. And my friends who are with me need to see her too! Please! It's very important!

TASH:
Wait here.
(*TASH goes off. Vanishes.*)

COLT:
You think we'll be allowed to see her?

LECK:
We better be! I hate to think we went through all that for nothing!

FOH:
I feel the same way.

LEEVUH (*Anxiously*):
She'll see us. She must!

[*TASH returns*.]

TASH:
Allright. You've been granted an audience with her.

LEEVUH:
Now?

TASH:
Yes.—But before you can all enter the City, you must wear these green shading lenses since its gem walls are blinding in sunlight.

FOH:
Splendor can blind I suppose.

LECK:
Yeah.
(*TASH hands out invisible green sunglasses which they all put on*.)

TASH:
You may come in now. Welcome to Emerald City. I'll take you to the Wizard's closed chamber. She's expecting you. Come!

[*The travellers follow her as they look about space in awe*.]

LEEVUH:
Because of these lenses, all of the people seem dressed in green as they stare at us. We probably look odd to them. We must stand out like sore thumbs! Everything looks green. The walls and buildings too. Look! Giant emeralds everywhere! See them?

COLT:
They're dazzling.

ZARNEY:
No dog biscuits? Forget it! You won't catch me being **GREEN** with envy!

LEEVUH:
Maybe not Toto—but I can't wait to go home.

COLT:
I wonder what this Wizard's like. I might be too scared to ask her for courage.

LECK:
And I want a heart.

FOH:
A brain.

LEEVUH:
It seems to me that at least at times everyone needs all those things.

TASH:
We're in the central palace now. The main hall. Go through those sliding doors. She's waiting for you. Now I'll leave you. Once you approach them, they'll automatically slide open for you to meet with her. Good luck.

COLT (*Fearfully*):
We'll need it!
(*TASH walks off. Vanishes.*)
I guess this is it. My knees are buckling. I think I'm too scared to go through with this.—to go in there to see I don't know what! Maybe I should forget it!—Just go back to my forest.—Live a cowardly life!

LEEVUH (*To COLT*):
That's not truly what you want, Fuhbby. Is it?

COLT (*Fearfully*):
Yes! No..Not really. It's just that I'm scared to death!

LEEVUH:
Have courage.

COLT:
That's just the trouble! I need it first.

LECK:
You've done too much for us already to be such a scare-dee cat!

LEEVUH (*Upbraiding LECK*):
Nick!
(*To COLT—*)
I'll tell you what. We'll all hold hands like we did in the woods and approach together.

COLT:
Okay!—But **don't** let go!

FOH:
None of us will.

LECK:
No.

ZARNEY:
WOOF!—**I** won't.

LEEVUH:
Ready?

COLT (*Terrified*):
..yeah..

[*They all walk slowly hand in hand to a certain point and then stop only to move forward again. They then all face the audience in a line and stare out as if looking at something horrible.*]

LECK:
What the heck is **that**?

COLT (*Trembling*):
I don't know..but it's scaring the life out of me! Excuse me while I cover my eyes!

FOH:

A dark giant flaming head?—Is **that** what she is?—the countenance of pure **nightmare**!

[*DAYJ as the Wizard now speaks to them from out of the dark. She is only a deep masculine* ***booming*** *voice from somewhere and cannot be seen.*]

DAYJ (*As Wizard*):

I AM OZ!

COLT (*Trembling*):

Cripes!

DAYJ (*Booming*):

I KNOW WHAT YOU WANT—*ALL OF* YOU SINCE I'M A WIZARD. BUT THERE IS A PRICE TO PAY. EVERYTHING IN LIFE HAS ONE. IF YOU WANT ME TO HELP YOU, YOU MUST HELP ME. THEREFORE DESTROY THE WITCH OF THE WEST! FOR,—SHE IS INTENSELY WICKED, SO DESERVES TO BE KILLED SINCE SHE THREATENED ME AND MY PEOPLE.

LECK:

But if you who are a powerful wizard can't do it, how do you expect **us** to?

DAYJ:

I DON'T KNOW BUT YOU MUST *KILL* HER! WHEN YOU HAVE DONE THAT, YOU CAN RETURN AND I'LL GRANT YOUR REQUESTS. NOT UNTIL THEN. NOW LEAVE ME. YOU HEAR? *GO*!!! I'M *FINISHED* WITH YOU.

COLT (*His hands are over eyes. Shaken*):

Is it gone?

FOH:

The face is gone. Yes.

LECK:

I guess we have to do what it says or give up on what we came for.

LEEVUH:

Kill the witch! I never voluntarily killed anyone or thing in my life and I don't want to start now. I don't believe in killing.

FOH:

I suppose we've no choice if we want the Wizard to send you home, Dorothy. I don't want to kill either. Having a brain isn't worth the destruction of a life no matter how evil it is but what else can we do?

LECK:

Is killing an evil being heartless? Is that the only way for me to get a heart? I don't know.

COLT:

I may be a coward but not to the point of committing murder and yet Dorothy can't go home otherwise like you pointed out, Blue. But maybe not all killing is a cowardly act especially in **this** case. **You** decide, Dorothy. We'll just go along with you.

ZARNEY:

I'm all for that. I would never leave you, Dorothy—no matter what your decision.

LEEVUH:

I know, Toto. Allright—we'll seek her out. We'll find the Witch of the West and kill her, but only if we have to.

COLT:

How do we do that? Where is she?

[*TASH approaches.*]

TASH:

I overheard you. The Witch of the West lives where **else**,—but in the west. She controls winged monkeys and a people called the Winkies. Just keep heading west throughout Oz. She lives in a dark castle there—although all dark souls don't neccessarily live in dark places. I've got to get back to the gates.

(*TASH exits.*)

COLT:

I guess that's what we'll do then.—Travel into the west. You guys ready? Dorothy?

LEEVUH:

Yes.

COLT:

Then let's all go.

[*They begin walking west,—symbolized by a circular path until they vanish into darkness*.]

SCENE FIVE:

[*Immediately afterward VORTEX as the western witch stops at center. She is in total dark but a light is on her*.]

VORTEX (*Angrily*):

My whole life I've been stepped on in different ways..hurt, deceived and betrayed..walked out on..rejected. **Abused**. **Laughed** at. I once had a husband but yes, he walked out on me too. **Every**one walks out on me. Everyone abandons me. Why was I born?—For nothing!—Nothing but rejection and pain..being treated like the most vile outcast! I had a good mother but she died when I was young, and ever since then I've been cheated by life. I don't get things in life that other people do..recognition. Happiness. My life's worth nothing then. Well, I'm **tired** of it! **TIRED**. Do you hear me? Do you hear me, God? I want things out of life. I want **good** things that I've been denied. I was born—so I'm worth it..Just by the fact of my birth. I was an innocent child once myself, so I've the right to some happiness. I don't deserve to be treated like a pariah.—Just trapped in a corner by life like some worthless insentient street garbage—not amounting to anything. I want **power**! I want a place in the sun! I wanna **be** somebody. Power—**yes**. My sister got those magic Silver Shoes initially because she was favored by my parents who gave her practically all their love!—But **I** deserve them.—Those shoes. I'm a worthwhile human being. I want them. I want those shoes! I want to experience their magic. I want real magic in my life! Who doesn't? Who doesn't want or need love? Everyone does. I want those **shoes** and I'm going to get them! My sister's **dead** after that girl landed on her with that house!—So they belong to **me**—not **her**! They're

VORTEX (*Cont'd*)**:**

my inheritance. I'm going to bring that girl to me who's wearing those shoes unrightfully and make sure she gives me what I'm owed.—Those **shoes**! I have the cap of the winged monkeys I acquired which controls the whole band. I'll have it bring her to me. That's right. That's right—bring her to me! She'll either give me those shoes or I'll **DESTROY** her! I want happiness. I want happiness at last. I've never truly been happy. Those shoes with all their magic will make me so. The Winkies don't. They don't love me. They obey my orders just because they fear me—fear the evil witch! Well who wouldn't wind up evil after what's been done to me? Who **wouldn't**, God? **TELL** ME! You have nothing to say about that, **do** you! God is always silent it seems when His children are in **PAIN**..and I'm His child too! I'm in pain! Neeko..Neeko—Come in here!

[*TASH enters flapping her arms like a winged monkey.*]

TASH (*Right before VORTEX*):
Yes Mistress?

VORTEX:

Go into the forest near me.—The darkest part of it which is all I've been given..no real light. Go in there with your army of winged monkeys. I happen to know there are travellers in it heading toward me. There's a girl with them..a little girl and her dog. I tried to destroy the others with my wolves, bees and crows but was unsuccessful. They slaughtered them. Use your army to somehow do away with the others except for the lion since he's the only one I can use for work but bring her to me—the girl. Carry her, her dog and the lion through the sky if you must but bring her. Understand? Do it **now**. At **once**. I can't go without those shoes for another second!

TASH (*As winged monkey King*):
Yes Mistress. I will obey.

VORTEX:
Good. I now have to tend to something. Be on your way.

[*Both move off in opposite directions into darkness.*]

SCENE SIX:

[*LEEVUH and her friends walk into sight.*]

LEEVUH (*As Dorothy*):
The trees are twisted. It's so dark here. We've been walking virtually for days it seems. You see that?—Up in the sky?

[*They all stop and look up.*]

ZARNEY:
WOOF! What is it? What are they?

LEEVUH:
They look like—yes—huge winged monkeys! Thousands of them! Run! They're coming down to attack us! Lion, don't stand there. There are too many so you can't protect us now. You'll only get yourself killed! Come-on!

[*The travellers including COLT flee off together into dark.*]

SCENE SEVEN:

[*VORTEX as the western witch comes into view. She begins pacing restlessly, briefly when TASH as Neeko joins her who pushes LEEVUH and ZARNEY before her into the presence of VORTEX.*]

VORTEX (*To TASH*):
Good! You brought them to me. What did you do with the lion?

TASH:
He proved himself difficult, Mistress. So he's in a cage in the courtyard. We locked him up so you can put him to work.

VORTEX:
Fine. You may go. Leave me with these. If I need you or your army again, I'll summon you.

TASH:
Verywell.
(*TASH walks off into dark.*)

ZARNEY (*Angrily at VORTEX*):
WOOF! WOOF! WOOF!

VORTEX (*To LEEVUH*):
Silence your dog or I'll kill him. Don't doubt my word.

LEEVUH:
Toto, be quiet.
[*VORTEX passes slowly back and forth near LEEVUH and ZARNEY as she intently glares at LEEVUH with the gaze of a cobra.*]

LEEVUH (*Cont'd*):
What will happen to my other two friends? Your monkeys destroyed them.

VORTEX:
They're no concern of mine. They're not fit to work so I had them eliminated. I want those shoes. They're not yours. They belonged to my sister. They're mine now since your house killed her. Take them off and give them to me at once!

LEEVUH:
I'm sorry your sister was killed by my house but the Northern Witch told me not to.

VORTEX:
She had no right to say that. They're mine. Take them off immediately or I'll harm you!

ZARNEY (*Outraged*):
WOOF! WOOF!

LEEVUH:
Toto, hush. I won't give them to you. The kiss of the northern witch and these shoes are the only things protecting me.

VORTEX:
Yes. I can see her shining mark on you. But your **dog** isn't protected. Suppose I kill him unless you just hand them over?

LEEVUH:
You'd kill Toto?

VORTEX:
In a heartbeat. I've the power to unless you give me those shoes.

LEEVUH (*Defeated*):
Allright.

VORTEX:
Now you're being smart.

ZARNEY:
Dorothy, don't give them to her! We'll be at her mercy otherwise.

LEEVUH:
I'm sorry, Toto. I have no choice. I love you too much.
(*LEEVUH reluctantly, fearfully removes the invisible shoes and hands them over to VORTEX.*)
Here.

VORTEX (*Smiling as she puts them on*):
You've made a wise decision. There! Yes! Already I feel their power flowing through me. At last I'm going to be happy. God has made me happy at last! Happy! Yes! I'm going to put them to use right **now**!
(*She turns to swiftly walk off into dark. She vanishes.*)

LEEVUH (*Watching*):
Watch out! Look where you're stepping. There's a floorwell of water before you!

VORTEX (*Unseen. In dark*):
Damn! I can't keep my balance!—Like many can't regarding me. I'm falling! Water dissolves me!

LEEVUH:
Come on, Toto! We've got to save her!
(*LEEVUH and ZARNEY race off into dark to save VORTEX.*)

VORTEX (*Crying out in terror*):
AHHHHHHHHHHHH!! **AHHHHHHHH**!!

SCENE EIGHT:

[*TASH as Neeko, FOH, COLT, LECK, ZARNEY and LEEVUH emerge from dark into view.*]

TASH (*To LEEVUH*):
Dead. Dead at last. The western witch is dead, so I and my monkey army are now free of her while the Winkies she enslaved are because of their new freedom, overjoyed. Thank you for helping us. After she died when you put those shoes back on as they floated in her wellwater which she otherwise so fearfully avoided, the Winkies as you know found in gratitude the ruined bodies of your tin and straw friends and restored them so they are now sound obviously and with you again.

LECK:
Yeah. It's otherwise awful to have a monkey on your back of any kind.

COLT:
The Winkies also freed me from that cage she had me in. She wanted me to work for her but I would never have done it knowing what at her hands might've happened to you and Toto even if that meant she'd see to it that I'd otherwise starve in there.

LEEVUH:
Thank Heavens you didn't, Lion but I never killed her though. She died accidentally. In fact I tried to save her while hoping that things would somehow work out for the best. For,—no matter what any soul goes through including me—that's all we can do. Hope.

COLT:
Right.

LEEVUH:
In spite of how she treated Toto and I, I'm sorry about the witch. Regrets are pointless though. Yet I'm sure God will have mercy on her soul. All we can do now is return to the Wizard to tell her what happened, so she can help us all. At least I hope she will, being that we didn't actually kill the witch.

TASH:

Allright. I and my monkey army would be happy then in our freedom to fly all your friends to Emerald City so you can do that.

LEEVUH:

Would you? We'd be grateful!

LECK:

We sure would. Having a monkey on my back under those conditions would be a relief.

TASH:

Then come with me now to the courtyard—all of you and I'll summon my band.

LEEVUH:

Thank you, Neeko. Thanks very much!

TASH:

No problem. Let's go.

[*TASH as Neeko gestures for all to follow her. They walk off into dark.*]

SCENE NINE:

[*LEEVUH, ZARNEY, FOH, LECK and COLT emerge from dark to face the audience. They are in the Wizard's throne room. The voice of DAYJ as the Wizard booms loudly at them. But again she is unseen.*]

DAYJ (*As Wizard*):

YOU'VE RETURNED I SEE. DID YOU KILL HER?

LEEVUH:

She died accidentally. I wear the shoes. I know we didn't destroy her but please!—will you now still help us?

DAYJ:

I'LL THINK IT OVER. COME AGAIN ANOTHER DAY.

LEEVUH (*Angrily*):

What do you mean? You said that if she was killed, you'd help us! I want to go home!

DAYJ:

I'M BUSY. YOU'LL HAVE TO COME BACK LATER.

COLT (*Savagely*):

ROARRRR! You know what we went through? If you had the slightest notion, you'd keep your word!

LECK (*Angry*):

Yeah! You don't make us go through hell like that and not keep it—you big phoney baloney!

DAYJ:

I'M NO PHONEY!

LECK:

Yes you **are**! Otherwise you'd keep your promise!

DAYJ:

DOROTHY DIDN'T ACTUALLY KILL THE WITCH, SO I'M UNDER NO OBLIGATION.

LECK:

You know what that is?—A "cop-out". You're just trying to weasel your way out of this. You know what **I** think? I think you have no power at all. You're a bigfat fraud! There's a lot of souls like you in the world who out of their own selfish needs make promises they don't keep. It's terrible to break promises because people put faith in them after everything they do because of them, so it's one of the worst things anyone can do—To break a promise—especially to a trusting innocent little child and her dog. Dorothy needs your help. We **all** do. But especially **her**!

ZARNEY (*Upset*):

WOOF!

FOH:

That's right!

COLT:
Yeah!

[*Suddenly DAYJ herself in person comes shamefully, slowly out from dark.*]

DAYJ (*Remorsefully*):
Hello?

[*They all turn to her.*]

ZECK:
Who are **you**?

DAYJ (*Shamefully*):
I'm the wizard.

ZECK:
An ordinary person? You're kidding!

FOH:
You're the Wizard?

DAYJ:
The only one. Look—I know you're all disappointed but I've got to be honest with you.—In terms of their morals and values..their integrity, I expect a lot from people since spiritually I want them to tow the line because God, I feel, needs that, whatever His agenda since He created us, but the truth is that in the end people are only human. They must be allowed to be so, as **I am** very fallibly I admit because I wanted you to do my dirtywork since I was incapable of it. You're right. I have no power. Technically in fact I am what is known as a humbug. A fraud. I look in my mirror and try to tell myself otherwise but I know the truth. I'm nothing but a phoney. A weak phoney. I had you do what I couldn't because I was terrified of that witch not only for me but for my people. No,—I really can't help you but please forgive me. Please! Please../The only reason everyone thinks I'm a wizard is because they were fascinated by how in Oz I arrived and because of how different I look. I came here accidentally by balloon from a circus in America where I once worked. I supervised the building of this city with my how should I say?—charisma—upon landing here and then sort of walled

DAYJ (*Cont'd*):

myself up inside it—in this palace—hidden from view so that no-one would discover what I truly am. Yes I'm a circus showman. I put on a good show with all the fireworks like that head I made which you saw. I somehow learned of what you all wanted before you first saw me. But how I did that isn't important. The thing is that what you all seek is somehow already inside you if you search in yourselves deeply enough. Life's storms like a devastating tornado will bring that out in you. Dorothy, you want to go home. That's all you want. But don't you see?—that because of your beautiful loving heart, your true home is inside you. That's right. You wouldn't even kill the witch. Home is only where love is which is in you. For, you can never really be home if you're not at peace with what's in your own heart—your own loving heart in your case. I've learned that. For, I can't be at peace with myself by living the life of a phoney indefinitely. I must be true to others but most of all myself. Lion—listen to me..You already have courage. Otherwise you wouldn't be able to help the others as you did. You have the same courage for your own dreams. Live them and whatever through them is in your heart and then you need not fear sleep.

LEEVUH:

You're right about Fuhbby. He was very protective of us and for that I love him and for his basic fragile humanness. I love you lion very much, you know. Very much! I really do!

LEEVUH (*To FOH*):

Your idea saved our lives in the poppy field. If you didn't already have a brain, Blue, you would never have been able to do that.

COLT:

I feel the same way about you, Kiddo.

DAYJ:

And **you** Scarecrow..You want a brain just to do good. But just **wanting** to do good shows you have a fine one spiritually. Not many people who have any sort of brain will even think about using it the way **you** want to.

FOH:

That didn't occur to me.

LEEVUH:
But it should have!

DAYJ:
And you—Tin Man—what a heart you have! Think about what you said to me to compel me to expose myself to you for what I really am..to get me to change. You value all lives above your own—especially when it comes to a little dog and the child he loves. You're truly altruistic.

LECK:
I have a real heart then? You really think so?

DAYJ:
Absolutely. If you doubt that, try stepping on even an ant and see how you react.

LECK:
My love isn't false then?

DAYJ:
No. It's the opposite.

LECK:
Then I'm very happy!

LEEVUH:
But still..Even after what you said about me, Wizard, I miss my Aunt Em. I miss Kansas. I forgive you but now I'll **never** be able to get back. I'm here in Oz for good! Aunt Em must be sick with worry about Toto and me, but there's nothing I can do! I miss Uncle Henry also!

COLT:
But we all love you too, Dorothy--even though you can't go back. We'll make a real home for you and Toto here. We'll do our very best to. Right guys?

LECK:
Yes!

FOH:
Definitely!

LEEVUH:
I appreciate that, truly..but as beautiful as Oz is in places, it just isn't Kansas. Understand? I love you all very much too. Yet Uncle Henry and Aunt Em mean everything to me. But I guess I'll never see them again!

FOH:
Look! You see that?

LECK:
What?

FOH:
A ball of light. A lovely woman is stepping out of it, pretty as an Angel.

[*TASH approaches LEEVUH out of dark.*]

LEEVUH:
Who are you?

TASH (*As Glinda*):
I'm Glinda..the Sorceress of the South. I know your plight, little Dorothy—but you needn't fret any longer. You've the power right now to return yourself and your dog to Kansas.

LEEVUH:
I do? What do you mean?

TASH:
Look to your feet.

LEEVUH:
My shoes?

TASH:
That's right.

COLT:
But if that's all it was, why didn't anyone tell her?

LECK:
Yeah.

FOH:
How come?

TASH:
It's something she needed to learn. In all we do or experience in life, we've got to find our own way home. What we are in ourselves is the only yellow brick road leading to it..to love and light. **Real** light. No matter what anyone does or says to you, you're not here to loathe yourself but to seek out light through love which will always lead you to your **real** Kansas..to your true Uncle Henry and Aunt Em. You understand?

LEEVUH:
I'll never be home and at peace unless I can really love and accept myself as a creation of God. If God didn't want me here, I wouldn't even exist.

TASH:
That's it.

COLT:
We should all have figured that out for her.

TASH:
No. This is something she had to see for herself. Now those magic shoes will send you home instantly. Both you and Toto.

LEEVUH:
Oh—I'm so happy! How wonderful! I can't believe it!

TASH:
Believe it, Dorothy. Believe in yourself like God who made you believes in **you**.

LEEVUH:

Yes. I'll remember! Well I guess this is goodbye. Goodbye Lion. I know things scare you sometimes but don't be afraid to be human. You've got plenty of courage. You just need to realize it.

COLT:

So do you, Dorothy. You helped me through it to be brave. I'll miss you a lot. My forest kingdom won't ever be the same without you.

[*She kisses him.*]

LEEVUH:

Keep your chin up and roar as loudly as you want for whatever reason because you're a free spirit! A lion!

COLT:

Okay. I will.

[*She hugs him.*]

LEEVUH:

And Scarecrow, I don't know where I'd be without you. You have a wonderful heart centered mind.

FOH:

No better than yours, Dorothy. Use yours wisely. Thinking about that will make me happy.

LEEVUH:

I'm glad. Goodbye Blue. (*She kisses and hugs FOH.*) And Nick—you've one beautiful heart. For, when you want a real heart so desperately, it means you already have one.

LECK:

I never told you, but when I was once a flesh and blood human, my heart was cut in two and now I fear the same thing's happening again.

LEEVUH:
Oh! Don't worry. It'll mend. Broken hearts always do at least eventually. Goodbye.

LECK:
Goodbye.

[*She kisses..hugs LECK.*]

LEEVUH:
Goodbye Wizard. Being true to yourself will make you true to others..just as you alluded to.

DAYJ:
I'll work on it.

LEEVUH:
Good. Well Toto, I guess we're ready to leave now.

ZARNEY (*Happy*):
WOOF!

LEEVUH:
He's anxious to go.

TASH:
You rcady?

LEEVUH:
Hold my hand, Toto.
(*He does.*)
Yes—I am.

TASH:
Now close your eyes, Dorothy—and tap your heels together three times as you think of all Home is to you. Think with your heart. Think of Home. Home.

[*LEEVUH closes her eyes as she holds ZARNEY's hand. All the others except for ZARNEY and herself move off into darkness.*]

LEEVUH (*Eyes closed*):
Home! Home!
(*She taps her heels together three times.*)
Home!

[*DAYJ returns running toward her. She is now Aunt Em. COLT runs along with her as Uncle Henry.*]

DAYJ:
Dorothy!
(*Embraces LEEVUH who opens eyes. DAYJ kisses her.*)
Dorothy! You're back!

LEEVUH (*Happily*):
Aunt Em!

ZARNEY (*Merrily*):
WOOF! WOOF!

DAYJ:
It's so good to have you back, darling—with Toto! Where have you been? Your Uncle Henry here and I have been frantic searching for you! We have for days!

COLT (*As Henry*):
Yeah hon' We have, baby. What happened to you? Because of the cyclone, we're living in a temporary dwelling until a new permanent one can be built.

LEEVUH:
Me and Toto—We've been trying to get home. It's a long story but it doesn't matter now. We're at last here with you both.—The one place that means everything to me. Home is where love is..where it's always somehow been even when I lost the sense of it because of things.
Like a single tiny shimmering star in a black starless night, love in this dark world is all that counts. Nothing matters more in our hearts nor in that of God Himself than love. That's right, Toto. LOVE.

ZARNEY:
Yes. LOVE.

[*The two hug eachother.*]

[*BLACKOUT.* ***THE END.***]

www.ingramcontent.com/pod-product-compliance
Ingram Content Group UK Ltd.
Pitfield, Milton Keynes, MK11 3LW, UK
UKHW051137260726
13967UKWH00010B/3101